D1060404

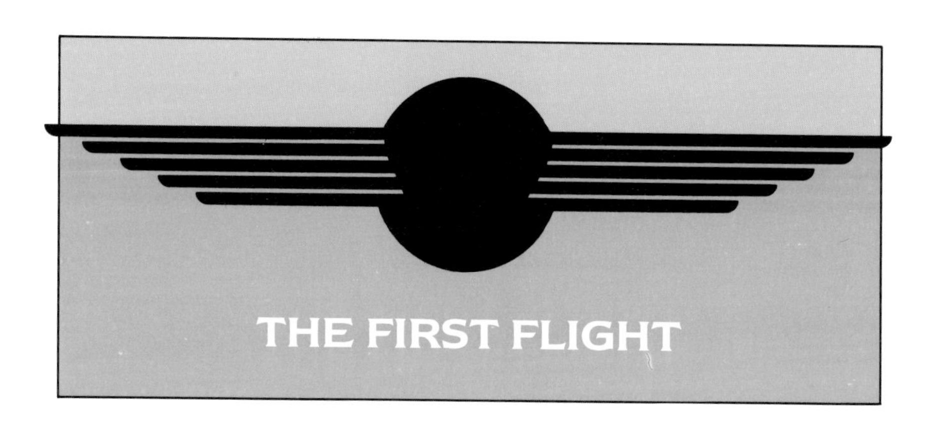
THE FIRST FLIGHT

THE FIRST

THE STORY OF
THE WRIGHT BROTHERS

RICHARD L. TAYLOR

Franklin Watts
New York / London / Toronto / Sydney / 1990
A First Book

Library of Congress Cataloging-in-Publication Data

Taylor, Richard L.
The first flight : the story of the Wright brothers /
by Richard L. Taylor.
p. cm. — (A First book)
Includes bibliographical references.
Summary: Describes how the Wright brothers developed the first airplane and places their achievement in the context of the aeronautic technology of the time.
ISBN 0-531-10891-0
1. Wright, Wilbur, 1867–1912—Juvenile literature. 2. Wright, Orville, 1871–1948—Juvenile literature. [1. Wright, Wilbur, 1867–1912. 2. Wright, Orville, 1871–1948. 3. Aeronautics—Biography.] I. Title. II. Series.
TL540.W7T38 1990
629.13'09—dc20
[920] 89-24774 CIP AC

Printed in the United States of America
6 5 4 3 2 1

This book is dedicated to
Jo Osborne, children's librarian
at the Worthington, Ohio,
public library. Without her
insistence and encouragement,
this project would never have
gotten off the ground.

Due to the fact that most of the photographs are copies of the original photos taken at the time, quality may vary.

Cover photograph courtesy of The Bettmann Archive

Photographs courtesy of:
The Bettmann Archive : pp. 10, 52 (bottom); Library of Congress: pp. 14 (top and bottom), 15 (bottom), 20, 21, 22, 23, 30 (top and bottom), 31 (bottom), 34, 35, 40, 41 (top), 44, 45, 50, 51, 52 (top and center); Smithsonian Institution: pp. 15 (top), 31 (top); Photo Researchers: pp. 21 (inset, Kenneth Murray), 56 (John Bova); Brown Brothers: p. 41 (bottom); The New York Public Library Picture Collection: p. 45 (inset); Smithsonian National Air Museum: p. 53; British Airways: p. 55.

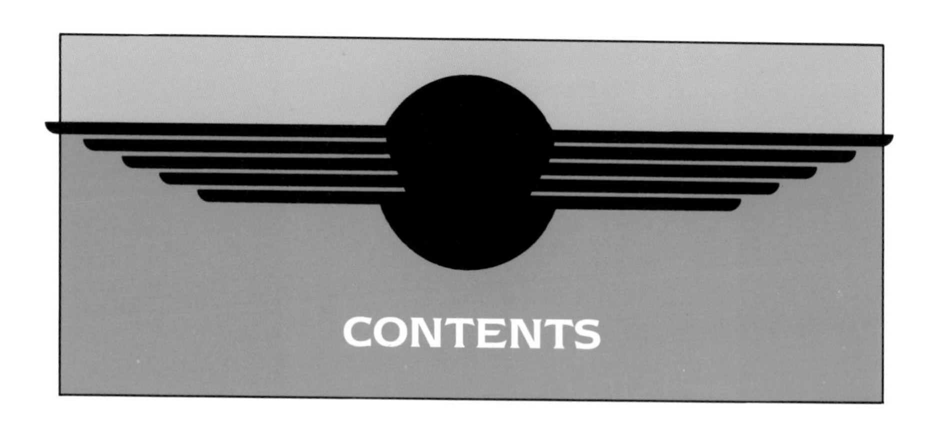
CONTENTS

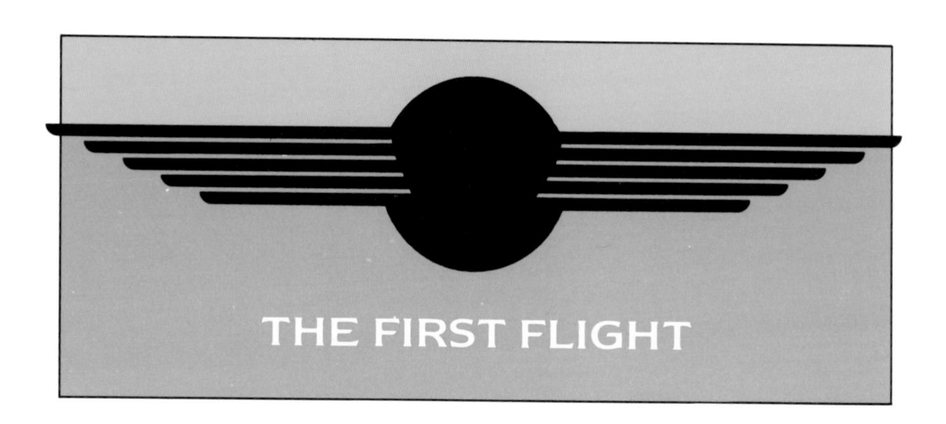
THE FIRST FLIGHT

For as long as records have been kept, people have wanted to learn to fly. This 1899 flying machine is but one example of what the human imagination has created.

THE PROBLEMS OF MANNED FLIGHT

In 1899 no one but birds and bees and bugs knew how to fly.

For hundreds of years—as long as records have been kept—humans have wanted to fly like birds. And for all that time, humans had tried to fly by imitating birds. They built wings and strapped them to their arms and then ran back and forth, flapping their wings as hard as they could, but they couldn't get off the ground.

Lightweight wings weren't nearly large enough to provide the necessary lift; and when the wings were made large enough, they were too heavy.

Humans were discovering that they couldn't imitate the flight of birds, which have very strong wing-flapping muscles and very light bodies. For a bird, flying is no more difficult than walking or running is for a human being.

In 1899, two young men who lived in Dayton, Ohio, became convinced that there must be a way for humans to fly.

Wilbur Wright and his brother, Orville, had spent many hours watching birds in flight, and they noticed that some of them were able to soar for long periods of time without flapping their wings. What was the secret of flight on motionless wings?

In May 1899, Wilbur wrote to the Smithsonian Institution in Washington, asking for any information they might have on the subject of flying.

In just a few days, the Wright brothers received a list of books and pamphlets, and discovered that a great number of inventors had tried to build flying machines. Nearly all of them had made the mistake of trying to copy birds—and none of them had even come close to flying. The Wright brothers realized that if they were going to fly, four major problems would have to be solved.

First, there was the matter of *lift*. The second problem was *control*—the ability to make the flying machine turn, climb, and descend. The brothers knew they would need a motor to turn propellers and push the machine through the air—*power* was problem number three. The fourth problem was actually learning how to fly, something that no human had ever done before.

The Wright brothers learned that curved wings, like those of the birds, apparently developed more lift than flat ones. A German experimenter named Lilienthal had tried very hard to understand the secrets of curved wings. Several years before the Wrights became interested in flight, Lilienthal had made more than 2,000 short flights from a hill near his home. His gliders were very small and had wings that looked like those of birds. Although these birdlike wings were able to support his weight quite well until he reached the bottom of the hill, they did not produce enough lift to allow him to fly level, much less gain any height.

Lilienthal tried to control his gliders by swinging his body to one side or the other. He discovered that he couldn't turn the glider very well at all. In August 1896 one of his flights ended in a shattering crash; lack of control cost Lilienthal his life.

Wilbur and Orville started with the information Lilienthal had discovered. By June 1899 they had built a double-winged glider, which they intended to fly as a kite. Now they had an opportunity to learn about lift and control with no danger to themselves. They reasoned that if they could make a set of wings that

Orville and
Wilbur Wright
in 1897.

The brothers were in the bicycle business in Dayton when they became interested in flying.

The German scientist Lilienthal also tried to fly, but one of his gliders crashed in 1896, killing him.

would develop lift and could be controlled, they would simply build bigger and bigger wings until they had a set large enough to lift a man.

The Wrights' first glider had two wings; each wing was 5 feet (1.5 m) long and 1 foot (.3 m) wide, with one wing set above the other. It was a wonderful kite, but a poor airplane, until Wilbur thought of a way to control it. He rigged a system of strings that caused the rear edges of the upper and lower wings on one side to be lowered, while the rear edges of the wings on the other side were raised. This twisting resulted in more lift on one side, which tilted the glider and made it turn in the opposite direction.

The strings were connected to wooden sticks—much like those of a modern controllable kite—and the Wrights were soon able to move their glider left and right as they wished. They had built a machine with enough lift to keep itself in the air, and had invented a simple system of control. It appeared that problems number one and number two had been solved.

2

A REAL-WORLD LABORATORY

It soon became clear to the brothers that if they followed their plan to build and fly bigger gliders, the fields around Dayton wouldn't be large enough. The flying machines they had in mind would need strong, steady winds, and when the kites became man-carrying gliders, they would want long, sloping hills with no trees or barns or fences in their way.

The United States Weather Bureau suggested they consider the Outer Banks of North Carolina.These long, narrow islands seemed perfect for the experiments. The wind off the ocean blew steadily almost all the time, and as far as you could see, there was nothing but gently sloping dunes and occasional large hills of soft sand.

Wilbur and Orville spent the winter of 1899 and the spring and summer of 1900 building a large glider, using the information from Lilienthal's experiments for the curvature of the wings.

Late that summer the Wrights took the glider apart, packed all the pieces and parts into a large shipping trunk, and set off for the village of Kitty Hawk, North Carolina.

They found the Outer Banks just as windy and sandy and deserted as they expected. The brothers set up camp, with a tent for themselves and their tools. Before long, their experiments were under way. Flying the glider as a kite, they added weight a little at a time, and soon came face to face with their first major disappointment—the glider would lift no more than 75 pounds (34 kg), and that was barely half the lift they needed.

After they changed the curvature several times, the wings developed enough lift to carry the brothers, one at a time, on short glides down the slope of a large sand dune. A small success, but there was hope. The brothers packed up and came home in October, their minds full of ideas for improving their flying machine.

Throughout the winter and spring of 1900–1901, the Wrights talked, thought, tested, and argued almost all the time about flying, trying to find out where their calculations had gone wrong. They were beginning to suspect that the curvature of the wings was at the heart of the problem.

The surf as it looked in October 1900 at Kitty Hawk, North Carolina, when the two Wright brothers arrived to test their glider. Inset: Sea oats and dunes at the Outer Banks of North Carolina.

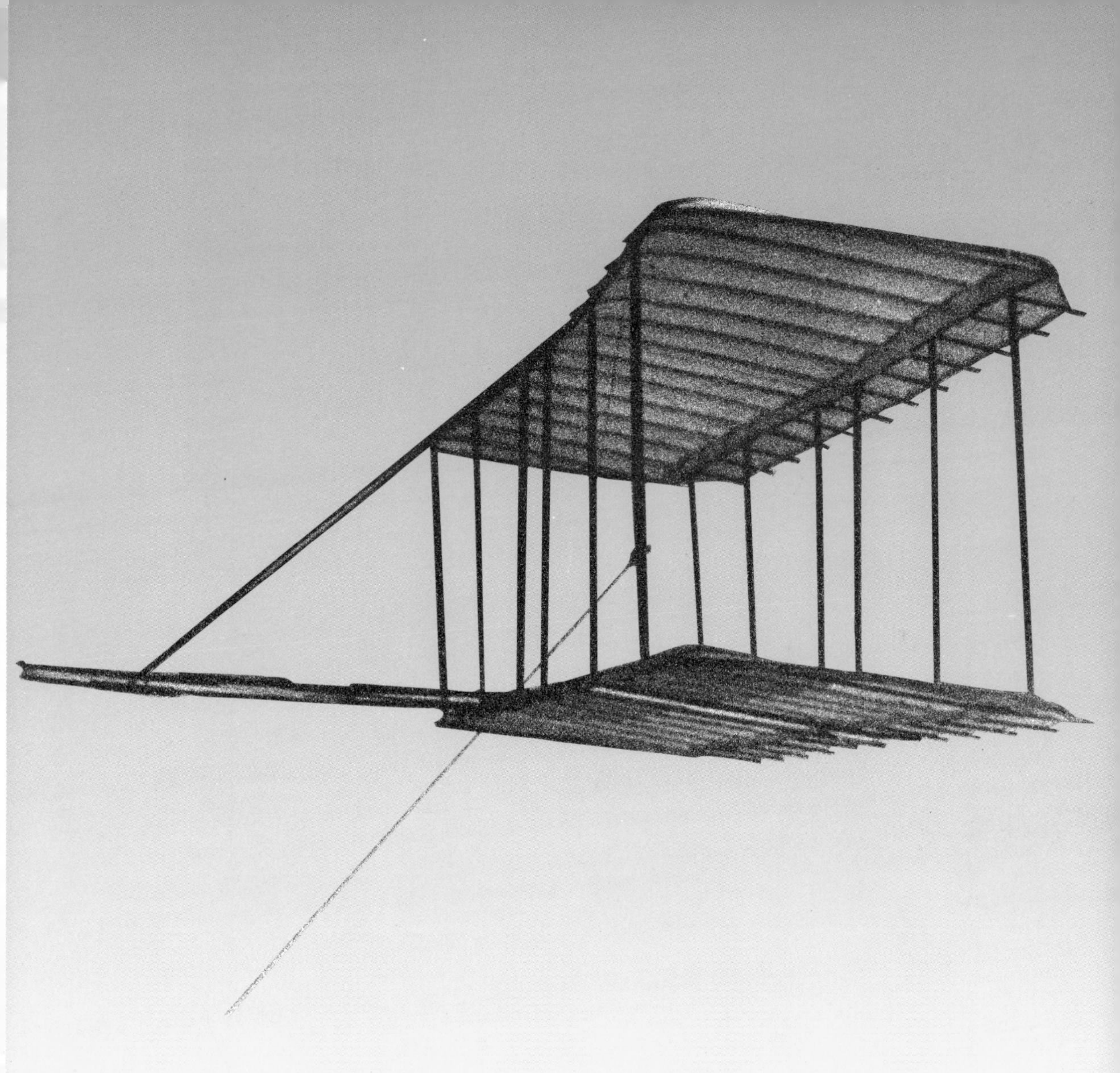

Once at Kitty Hawk, Orville and Wilbur set up camp in a tent on the dunes. Initially, the two men flew their glider as you would fly a kite.

HOW LIFT IS PRODUCED

When a flat wing is inclined a bit so that the wind strikes it at an angle, the air is deflected downward, and some of the pushing-back force turns into lift. But when that same flat wing is curved just a little bit, another force appears. The curved surface forces some air underneath, while the rest goes rushing across the top.

Because of the curve, the over-the-top air must travel a greater distance and must therefore speed up in order to reach the back of the wing at the same time as the air flowing underneath.

Whenever air is speeded up, its pressure is reduced. This means that as a curved wing moves through the air, there is less pressure on top of the wing. Now, with a difference in pressure, the curved wing—and everything attached to it, such as an airplane—is pushed upward.

4 THE RESEARCH CONTINUES

Knowing they had a great deal to learn about lift, wing curvature, and control, the Wrights returned to Kitty Hawk in July 1901. Their new glider had wings 22 feet (6.7 m) long and 7 feet (2.1 m) wide and which weighed almost 100 pounds (45 kg).

Like all the Wright flying machines, this one had a framework of wood, mostly spruce, all of it cut to shape, sanded, and varnished by the brothers themselves. The wings were covered with fine cloth, and were held several feet apart by thin upright pieces of wood at front and rear. The whole glider was held together with steel wires, drawn up tightly for strength while allowing the wings to flex for control.

The first few attempts to glide from the top of one of the large sand hills near their camp were very disappointing. Although they were able to control up and down motion and were able to keep the glider moving straight ahead by twisting the wings, neither Wilbur nor Orville could make the machine climb more than a few feet off the ground.

They had used Lilienthal's data to design the curvature of the wings, but the glider was not developing nearly enough lift. Could Lilienthal's numbers have been wrong? Would a change in wing curvature make a difference? There was only one way to find out.

On the last Saturday in July 1901, the brothers made another adjustment in the curvature of the wings, and once again carried the glider to the top of the sand hill.

Wilbur climbed aboard. Orville and a helper from the nearby village took their positions, one at each wing tip. On a signal, they ran down the slope, pulling the glider until it had enough speed to maintain itself in flight. And as if it had suddenly come alive, the glider soared out over the sand, gaining altitude and *flying*! The change in wing shape made all the difference in the world.

Now the Wrights turned their attention to the problem of control. Although they were able to keep the glider on a straight course as it flew downhill, they knew that a flying machine would be worthless unless the pilot could make it turn.

Very cautiously, the Wrights experimented with gentle turns to the left and right—and they ran head-on into a problem that had never entered their minds. As the glider was turned, it swung its nose in the opposite direction and began sliding sideways toward the ground. The lowered wing tip caught the sand, and sent man and machine cartwheeling across the beach.

Time after time, the Wright brothers soared out across the dunes, everything going well until they tried to turn. And then each time, the glider slid sideways, dug a wing tip into the sand, and slammed to a stop.

Two very discouraged brothers closed their camp on the North Carolina beach and headed home at the end of August 1901. It was clear that Lilienthal's calculations for the shape of a wing and its curvature were wrong. And on top of that, their method of wing-warping just wasn't working.

5 PICK UP THE PIECES AND CARRY ON

The brothers' depression didn't last long. Shortly after they were settled again in Dayton, they attacked the problem of building wings of the proper size and shape and with the right amount of curvature. This time, they started with their own ideas and built a small wind tunnel to test their theories.

All through the winter, Wilbur and Orville experimented with different sizes and shapes of wings. They developed the world's first accurate set of calculations for designing and building wings. They chose the best of more than two hundred wing shapes and sizes, and settled on the curvature that had produced the most lift in their homemade wind tunnel.

In 1901, the brothers returned to Kitty Hawk and attempted to fly a new, revised glider. After many attempts, the new glider actually soared and flew with Wilbur hanging on!

Back in Dayton, Orville and Wilbur built a wind tunnel to test their various theories about why their glider wouldn't turn.

Returning to the slope of Big Kill Devil Hill at Kitty Hawk in the late summer of 1902, the brothers now had a glider which they hoped would respond to turns. And, on October 2, 1902, the new machine responded well.

When the brothers arrived at Kitty Hawk on August 28, 1902, very little had changed on the deserted beaches, but there were big changes in the glider they brought with them for their third attempt to unlock the secrets of manned flight. The wings on the 1902 glider were based on the successful wind tunnel tests, and they had added a double vertical rudder behind the main wings to overcome the sideways slipping whenever the glider was turned.

By the end of October, when the Outer Banks weather was turning cold and too windy to fly, the Wrights had made more than a thousand flights down the sloping hills of sand, some of them for more than 600 feet (183 m), all of them under complete control. The glider responded quickly and positively as Wilbur and Orville operated the controls to turn left and right.

When they left for home in late October, the Wright brothers were certain that the problems of lift and control had been solved and that they had learned a great deal about how to fly. They knew that success was now only a matter of adding a motor to their glider.

6 ENGINE AND PROPELLERS —A REAL PROBLEM

The Wrights' next task seemed a simple one—find a motor that was light enough and powerful enough to get the glider off the ground. Their calculations showed that the motor could not weigh more than 180 pounds (81.6 kg), and that it would have to produce at least twelve horsepower, but there were no such motors available in 1902. So, rather than build a glider large enough to support a much heavier engine, they designed and built a motor of their own.

Neither Orville nor Wilbur had any formal education beyond high school. Yet in just three and one-half years—from 1899 when they wrote for information about flying until the autumn of 1902 when they had solved the problems of lift and control—Wilbur,

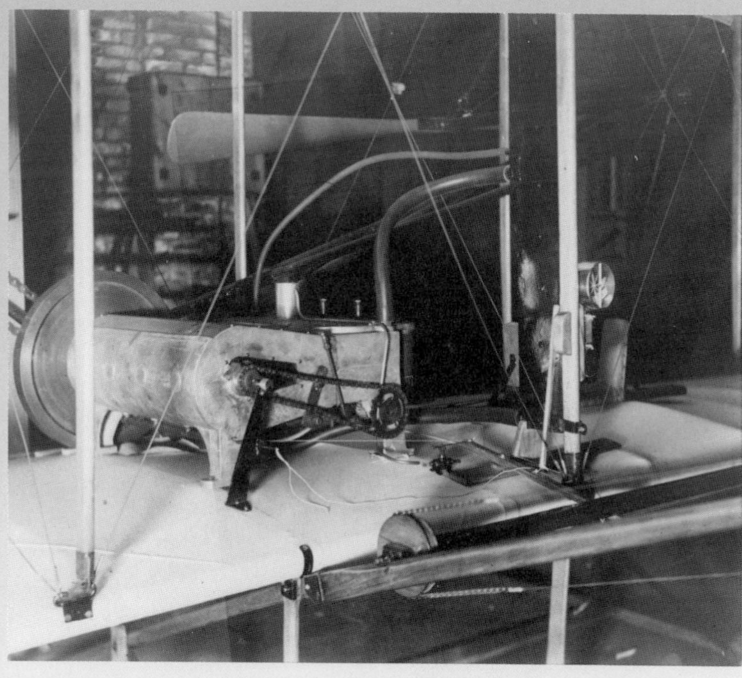

All the men needed now for their glider was a motor. So they built one themselves in their machine shop back in Dayton.

thirty-five years old, and Orville, thirty-one, had become the most knowledgeable people in the world about flying. They had surpassed the achievements of every would-be flyer since the beginning of time. They had not only discovered major errors in the theories of flight, they had also researched, tested, and *proved* that their own ideas were correct.

And now, faced with a problem that would have stopped many men of higher education, the brothers rolled up their sleeves and built an engine.

The next problem turned out to be the hardest of all. The Wrights knew that they needed a propeller—simply put, a large fan—that would move air backward and cause the flying machine to move forward.

Once again, Wilbur and Orville turned to existing technology. After all, air behaved much like water, and surely the makers of boat propellers knew everything about propeller design. The brothers were astounded to find out that marine engineers knew very little about how or why their propellers worked.

Yet another time, the Wrights studied, researched, tested, and tried until they came up with two-bladed wooden propellers that would generate enough thrust (push) to move the glider forward. They decided on two propellers turning in opposite directions so that the rotational force of one would cancel that of the other, and also because a single propeller large enough to do the job would be too big for their little engine to turn.

During the winter of 1902–1903, Wilbur and Orville worked on the machine that was to become the world's first airplane. Using the knowledge and experience they had gained from the successes of the previous summer at Kitty Hawk, they scaled up their glider drawings to accommodate the additional weight of the motor.

THE "WRIGHT FLYER" IS BORN

It was a "whopper flying machine," according to Wilbur. Twenty-one feet (6.4 m) long, wings stretching more than 40 feet (12.2 m) from tip to tip, the entire airplane weighed 605 pounds (274 kg). The pilot would lie on his stomach on the lower wing, with a lever to operate the elevator out front. Wires attached to a movable hip cradle twisted the wings to make the machine turn. As the pilot shifted his weight to the right or left, the wing twisted and the rudders moved simultaneously to prevent the nose from swinging in the wrong direction.

On September 23, 1903, the brothers left Dayton for their third trip to the Outer Banks. They were soon flying again, delighted to discover that they had not forgotten last year's lessons of aircraft control. When the wind was favorable, they practiced their flying skills in a glider. When the wind died or got too strong to fly, they worked on the powered machine.

Autumn turned to winter along the Outer Banks as the Wrights worked through November and into December. Strong winds and cold, raw days made life very uncomfortable, but the brothers had decided to stay until they had tried at least once to get their machine into the air.

The "Wright *Flyer,*" as the brothers named it, needed a strong, steady wind in order to fly, since the engine and propellers alone could not push it forward fast enough to generate sufficient lift. The wind and weather were perfect on December 13, and this day might have seen the First Flight. But it was Sunday, and the Wright brothers never worked on the Sabbath.

On Monday, there was a gentle breeze of only five miles per hour, not nearly enough to get the *Flyer* into the air from level ground. Still, the Wrights didn't want to miss a single opportunity to learn more about flying, so they set up their launching rail—a track made of 2″×4″ (5 cm × 10 cm) boards set on edge—on the side of a sand dune to take advantage of the slope.

The Wright brothers assembling the 1903 machine
in the new camp building at Kill Devil Hill.

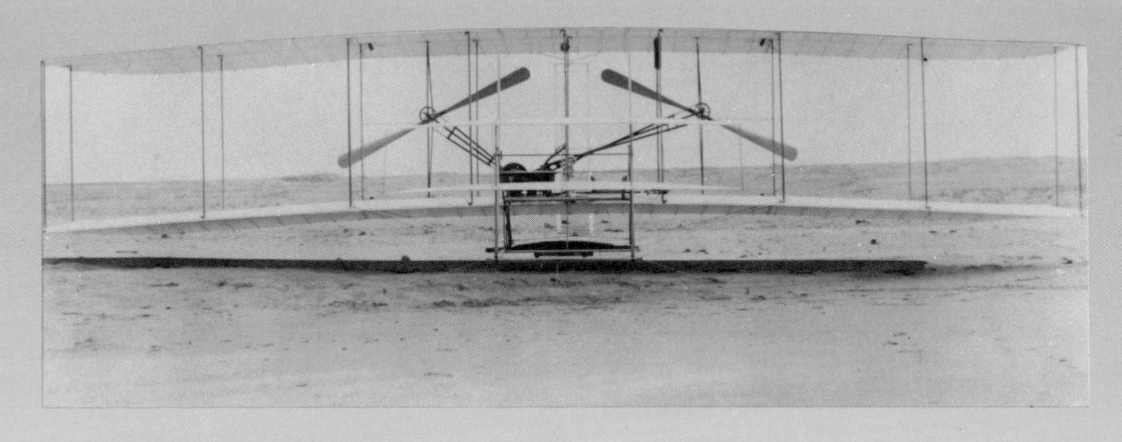

Front view of the finished plane.

Getting ready to take off!

The brothers tossed a coin for the honor of making the first try. Wilbur won and settled himself in the hip cradle on the lower wing. When the engine was running at full power with Orville holding a wing tip to balance the *Flyer* on the narrow rail, Wilbur released the wire that kept the airplane from moving.

After rolling forward 40 feet (12.2 m), the *Flyer* lifted off the track and climbed 15 feet (4.5 m) into the air—and almost immediately sank back onto the sand, catching a wing tip and cartwheeling to a stop, splintering several pieces of its wooden structure in the process.

What might have been the First Flight lasted just three and one-half seconds, and the *Flyer* lay damaged only 105 feet (32 m) from its starting point.

The brothers didn't consider this a success, since Wilbur had clearly overcontrolled the elevator, causing the nose to rise so sharply that the *Flyer* couldn't continue through the air. They had come very close.

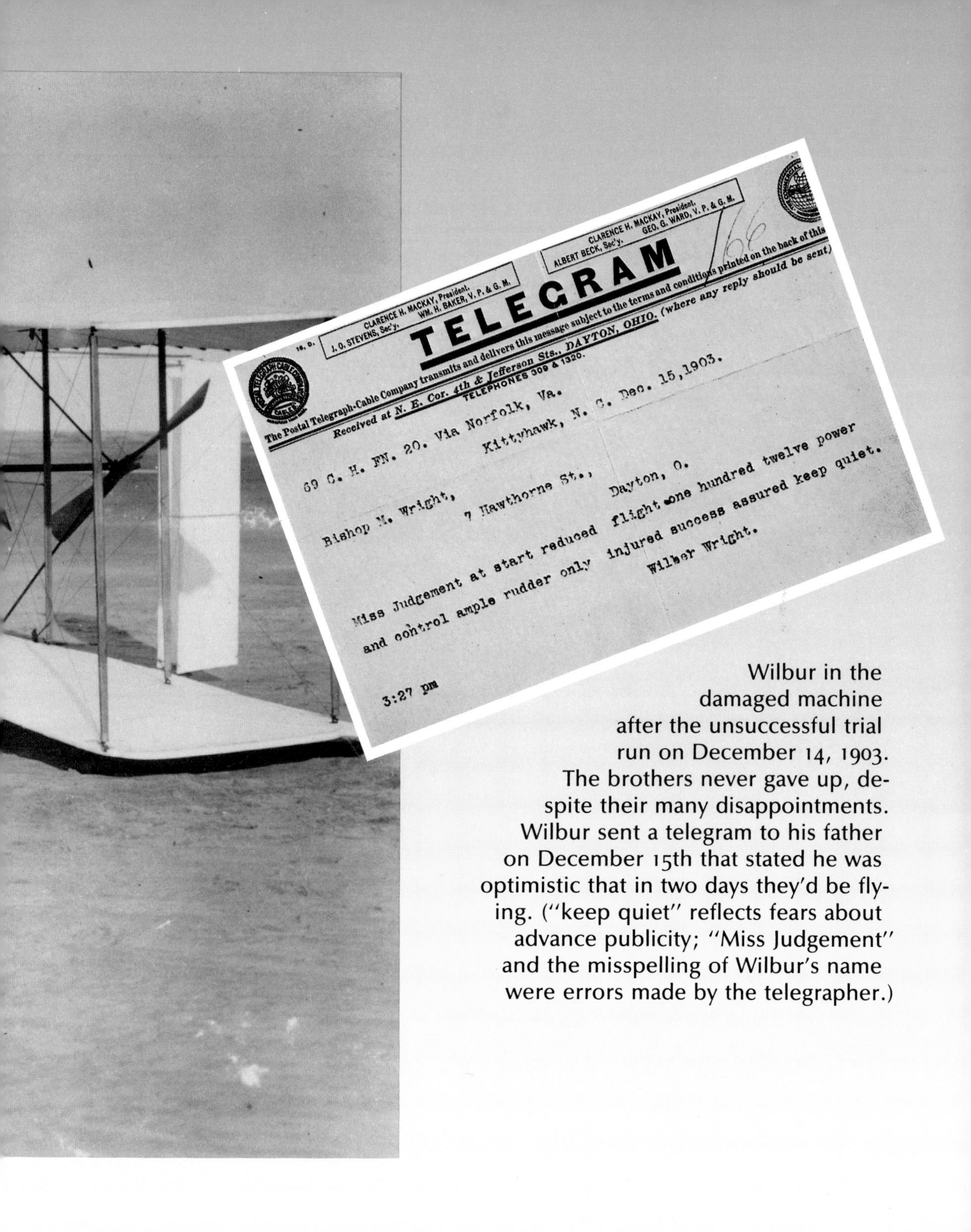

16. D.

CLARENCE H. MACKAY, President.
J. O. STEVENS, Sec'y. WM. H. BAKER, V. P. & G. M.

TELEGRAM

CLARENCE H. MACKAY, President.
ALBERT BECK, Sec'y. GEO. G. WARD, V. P. & G. M.

The Postal Telegraph-Cable Company transmits and delivers this message subject to the terms and conditions printed on the back of this

Received at N. E. Cor. 4th & Jefferson Sts., DAYTON, OHIO. *(where any reply should be sent)*

TELEPHONES 309 & 1320.

166

69 C. H. FN. 20. Via Norfolk, Va.

Kittyhawk, N. C. Dec. 15,1903.

Bishop M. Wright,

7 Hawthorne St.,

Dayton, O.

Miss Judgement at start reduced flight one hundred twelve power and control ample rudder only injured success assured keep quiet.

Wilber Wright.

3:27 pm

Wilber in the damaged machine after the unsuccessful trial run on December 14, 1903. The brothers never gave up, despite their many disappointments. Wilbur sent a telegram to his father on December 15th that stated he was optimistic that in two days they'd be flying. ("keep quiet" reflects fears about advance publicity; "Miss Judgement" and the misspelling of Wilbur's name were errors made by the telegrapher.)

In a letter to their family that night, Wilbur wrote, "The machinery all worked in entirely satisfactory manner, and seems reliable. The power is ample, and but for a trifling error due to lack of experience with this machine and this method of starting, the machine would undoubtedly have flown beautifully."

The *Flyer*'s broken skids and supports were quickly repaired, and Orville was ready for his turn the next day. December 15 might have been the day of the First Flight, but again, there was no wind.

December weather along the Outer Banks of North Carolina can change from beautiful to miserable overnight, and that is exactly what happened. The complete lack of wind on December 15th was replaced by a roaring storm the next day. The brothers didn't even consider taking their frail airplane out of its shed, for they knew it would be ripped apart by the strong winds.

NOW OR NEVER— CHRISTMAS IS COMING

When daylight came to Kitty Hawk on December 17, 1903, the weather hadn't changed at all. A solid layer of low clouds moved across the sands, pushed by a howling wind that occasionally reached a speed of 30 miles (48 km) per hour.

The Wrights now faced a dilemma. December storms on the Outer Banks sometimes lasted for weeks. They knew that they were very close to success, and they knew that if they didn't make another attempt soon, the First Flight would be postponed until spring. The brothers had promised their family that they'd be home for Christmas, and the Wright brothers were known for keeping promises.

At ten o'clock in the morning on that Friday, December 17, Wilbur and Orville made their decision. They raised a flag, a signal that summoned their helpers from the village, and they began setting up the starting track. Within thirty minutes, the *Flyer* was positioned on the track, its wings rocking in the gusty wind. Orville was so confident of success that he set up his camera to capture the First Flight on film, and he instructed one of the spectators to snap the shutter just as the *Flyer* passed the end of the track.

Orville settled into his position on the bottom wing, tested the controls, and made sure that everything was in order. He glanced to his right, where Wilbur steadied the wing. When he sensed that the engine was running as fast as it could, Orville pulled the release wire and the *Flyer* began rolling down the track.

With the help of a 27 mile (43 km) per hour wind, the *Flyer* lifted away from its dolly before it had moved forty feet (12.2 m). The nose of the airplane started to rise, and Orville pushed on the elevator control to bring it down. The elevator was too large and too sensitive, and Orville had to use full movement of the elevator control to keep the *Flyer* on a level path.

After 100 feet (30 m) of violent ups and downs, the airplane dipped its nose so far that Orville couldn't overcome it. The *Flyer* went another twenty feet before it skidded to a stop in the sand, but it had *flown*!

Only 120 feet (36 m), only twelve seconds in the air, but Orville had done it! He had flown the airplane from a standstill under its own power, he had maintained control long enough to prove that it could be done, and he had landed the *Flyer* safely.

Orville was able to help his brother understand how to handle the oversized elevator, and in less than an hour, Wilbur was ready for the next attempt. The howling wind and freezing temperature didn't matter anymore—the Wright brothers were *flying*!

At 11:20 that morning, Wilbur completed a flight of 175 feet (53 m) in twelve seconds. Twenty minutes later, Orville tried again, and this time, he stayed in the air for fifteen seconds and flew 200 feet (61 m) across the sand.

On the fourth attempt, the *Flyer* behaved just as it had on the other flights, bucking up and down as Wilbur fought the combination of wind gusts and the super-sensitive elevator. But he kept the *Flyer* in the air for 300 feet (91 m). Sometimes as high as fifteen feet (4.6 m), never lower than eight feet (2.4 m) above the ground, Wilbur continued until a strong gust of wind and the elevator control problem finally got the best of him. But he had traveled 852 feet (260 m) and had flown for nearly a full minute!

The world's First Flight had taken place on Friday, December 17, 1903.

The First Flight was recorded on December 17, 1903, as the Wright brothers' glider flew 120 feet in twelve seconds with Orville at the controls. Orville and Wilbur Wright had finally done it!

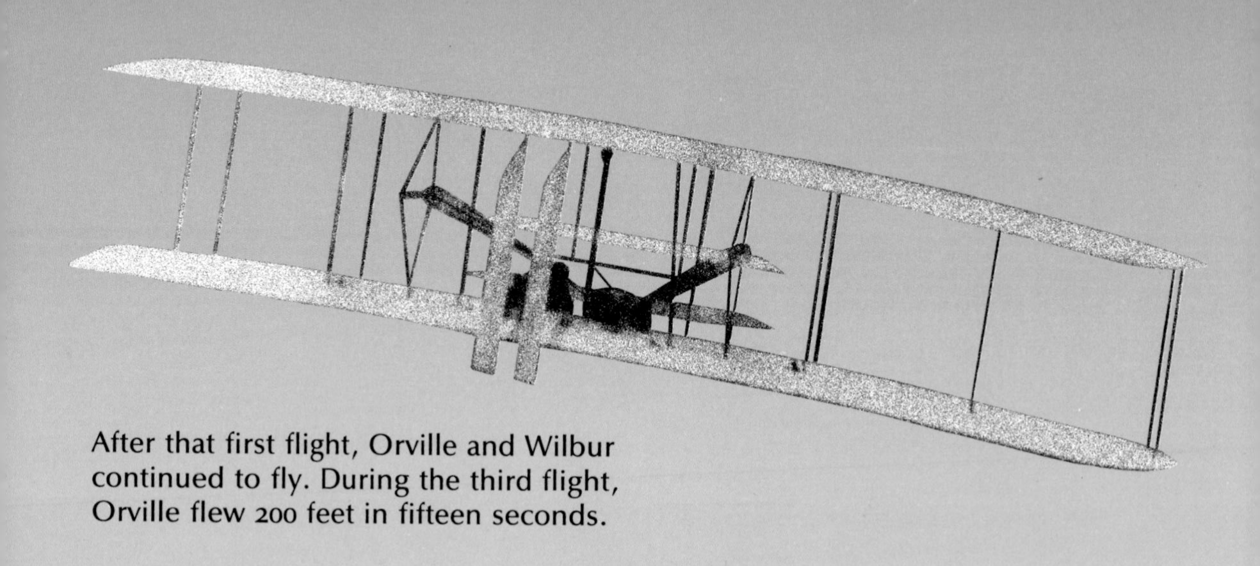

After that first flight, Orville and Wilbur continued to fly. During the third flight, Orville flew 200 feet in fifteen seconds.

What the machine looked like at the end of the last flight; its rudder frame broke in the landing.

12 Pages

Virginian-Pilot.

THREE CENTS PER COPY.

FLYING MACHINE SOARS 3 MILES IN TEETH OF HIGH WIND OVER SAND HILLS AND WAVES AT KITTY HAWK ON CAROLINA COAST

NO BALLOON ATTACHED TO AID IT

TALLY SHEETS WILL DECIDE CONTEST

U. S. LANDING PARTY FINDS STRONG CAMP OF COLOMBIAN TROOPS

TO DEEPEN THE HARBOR AT NORFOLK

"WANTS CANAL BUILT WITHOUT SUSPICION OF NATIONAL DISHONOR"

Three Years of Hard, Secret Work by Two Ohio Brothers Crowned With Success

ACCOMPLISHED WHAT LANGLEY FAILED AT

An original account of the earliest human flight in all time. From the Norfolk, Virginia, *Virginian-Pilot*, December 18, 1903, the day after the historic event.

Orville and Wilbur Wright.
The present state of flight would not have been possible without their determination, drive, and perseverance.

In the years since that first flight, airplanes have developed at an incredible pace: the comfort, speed, and safety of aviation today were surely beyond the Wright brothers' wildest dreams. But no matter how fast, no matter how big, no matter how powerful the airplanes we use today, they are all direct descendants of that fragile, white-winged glider-with-a-motor that was the first successful powered airplane.

In 1903, only nature's creatures knew how to fly; but in December of that year, birds and bees and bugs were joined by *brothers*. The First Flight was indeed a great moment in aviation.

The Concorde. We have come a long, long way since that triumphant day in 1903 at Kitty Hawk, North Carolina.

The Wright Brothers Memorial at Kill Devil Hill, Kitty Hawk, North Carolina.

Wilbur Wright

Born: April 16, 1867 on a farm near Millville, Indiana

Died: May 30, 1912 in Dayton, Ohio

Orville Wright

Born: August 19, 1871 at 7 Hawthorne Street, Dayton, Ohio

Died: January 30, 1948 in Dayton, Ohio

The *Kitty Hawk Flyer*
The world's first successful airplane

First (and only) flights took place on December 17, 1903, at Kitty Hawk, North Carolina. The *Flyer* was wrecked by a gust of wind following the fourth flight on that day. It was disassembled, shipped to Dayton, and placed in storage. In 1928, Orville Wright loaned it to the Science Museum in South Kensington, London, England.

The *Flyer* was returned to the United States in 1948, and was placed on display in the Smithsonian Institution's Hall of Aviation. Today, it occupies a place of honor in the National Air and Space Museum in Washington, D.C.

A replica of the *Flyer* may be seen in the Wright Brothers National Memorial at Kill Devil Hills, North Carolina, adjacent to the site of the First Flight. The Memorial contains Wright memorabilia and replicas of the brothers' 1903 living quarters and hangar/workshop.

Greenfield Village in Dearborn, Michigan, contains the Wright Brothers' original bicycle shop. This original building also contains much of the original machinery the brothers used in making their *Flyer*. Greenfield Village also has the brothers' homestead, the house in which Orville was born. There are displays of later Wright airplanes and other memorabilia in the Air Force Museum in Fairborn, Ohio, and at Wright Hall in Carillon Park, Dayton, Ohio.

A piece of the *Flyer*'s original linen wing fabric was carried to the moon by Neil Armstrong on his historic space flight in July 1969.

Specifications

Weight—605 pounds (274 kg) without pilot

Length—21 feet (6.7 m)

Wingspan—40 feet, 4 inches (12.2 m)

Wing surface area—512 square feet (47.5 sq m)

Propellers—Two counter-rotating "airscrews," each 8.5 feet (2.6 m) in diameter. The propellers were made of three laminations of spruce wood, covered with canvas to prevent splintering, then painted with aluminum paint. The propellers turned at a speed of approximately 330 revolutions per minute and produced 90 pounds (41 kg) of thrust.

Engine—Four horizontal opposed cylinders made of cast iron. This was a "square" engine, with four-inch bore and stroke, and a displacement of 201 cubic inches (3,294 cu cm). It produced approximately 12 horsepower (9 kw).

Flight controls—The Wrights lay prone on the lower wing, and by moving their hips to left or right operated the wing-warping mechanism and the rear-mounted vertical rudders. The horizontal elevators, well out ahead of the wings, were moved up and down by a lever in the pilot's left hand.

Statistics of the flights

First flight (Orville)—120 feet (36 m), 12 seconds

Second flight (Wilbur)—175 feet (53 m), 12 seconds

Third flight (Orville)—200 feet (61 m), 15 seconds

Fourth and final flight (Wilbur)—852 feet (260 m), 59 seconds

The *Flyer* was rebuilt for display, but never flew again.

FOR FURTHER READING

Bendick, Jeanne. *Airplanes*. New York: Franklin Watts, 1982.

Hosking, Wayne. *Flights of Imagination: An Introduction to Aerodynamics*. National Science Teachers Association, 1987.

Jefferis, David. *The First Flyers*. New York: Franklin Watts, 1988.

Reynolds, Quentin. *The Wright Brothers*. New York: Random House, 1981.

Robins, Jim. *The Story of Flight*. New York: Warwick Press, 1986.

Rosenblum, Richard. *Wings, the Early Years of Aviation*. New York: Four Winds Press, 1980.

Sobol, Donald. *The Wright Brothers at Kitty Hawk*. New York: Scholastic, 1987.

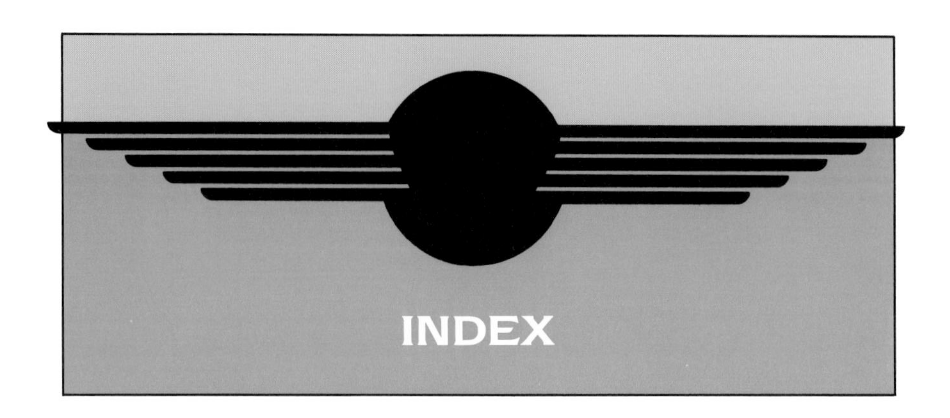

Page numbers in *italics* indicate illustrations.